CAROLINA COOKBOOK

A SOUTHERN COOKBOOK WITH AUTHENTIC NORTH CAROLINA RECIPES AND SOUTH CAROLINA RECIPES FOR EASY SOUTHERN COOKING

By
BookSumo Press
Copyright © by Saxonberg Associates

Published by
BookSumo Press, a DBA of Saxonberg Associates
http://www.booksumo.com/

ABOUT THE AUTHOR.

BookSumo Press is a publisher of unique, easy, and healthy cookbooks.

Our cookbooks span all topics and all subjects. If you want a deep dive into the possibilities of cooking with any type of ingredient. Then BookSumo Press is your go to place for robust yet simple and delicious cookbooks and recipes. Whether you are looking for great tasting pressure cooker recipes or authentic ethic and cultural food. BookSumo Press has a delicious and easy cookbook for you.

With simple ingredients, and even simpler step-by-step instructions BookSumo cookbooks get everyone in the kitchen chefing delicious meals.

BookSumo is an independent publisher of books operating in the beautiful Garden State (NJ) and our team of chefs and kitchen experts are here to teach, eat, and be merry!

INTRODUCTION

Welcome to *The Effortless Chef Series*! Thank you for taking the time to purchase this cookbook.

Come take a journey into the delights of easy cooking. The point of this cookbook and all BookSumo Press cookbooks is to exemplify the effortless nature of cooking simply.

In this book we focus on Carolina. You will find that even though the recipes are simple, the taste of the dishes are quite amazing.

So will you take an adventure in simple cooking? If the answer is yes please consult the table of contents to find the dishes you are most interested in.

Once you are ready, jump right in and start cooking.

— BookSumo Press

TABLE OF CONTENTS

Any Issues? Contact Us

If you find that something important to you is missing from this book please contact us at info@booksumo.com.

We will take your concerns into consideration when the 2nd edition of this book is published. And we will keep you updated!

— BookSumo Press

LEGAL NOTES

COMMON ABBREVIATIONS

cup(s)	C.
tablespoon	tbsp
teaspoon	tsp
ounce	oz.
pound	lb

*All units used are standard American measurements

Chapter 1: Easy Carolina Recipes

Carolinian Chicken

Ingredients

- 6 C. water
- 1 tbsp salt
- 1 onion, chopped
- 1 (3 lb.) whole chicken
- 3 1/2 C. chicken broth
- 1 C. long-grain white rice
- 1/2 lb. smoked sausage of your choice, sliced
- 2 tbsp Italian-style seasoning
- 2 cubes chicken bouillon

Directions

- In a large pan, add the water, salt, onion and chicken and bring to a boil.
- Cook for about 1 hour.
- Transfer the chicken into a plate and keep aside to cool.
- Remove the skin and bones of the chicken.
- Chop the remaining meat into bite size pieces.

- With a slotted spoon, skim off the fat from the chicken broth.
- In a 6-quart pan, add about 3 1/2 C. of the chicken broth, rice, chicken pieces, sausage, herb seasoning and bouillon and cook for about 30 minutes.
- Reduce the heat to low and simmer, covered till the desired consistency, stirring occasionally.

Amount per serving (6 total)

Timing Information:

Preparation	30 m
Cooking	1 h
Total Time	2 h

Nutritional Information:

Calories	726 kcal
Fat	43 g
Carbohydrates	29.8g
Protein	50.9 g
Cholesterol	198 mg
Sodium	2756 mg

* Percent Daily Values are based on a 2,000 calorie diet.

SHRIMP DINNER

Ingredients

- 3 slices bacon
- 1 onion, chopped
- 1 green bell pepper, seeded and chopped
- 2 tsp seasoned salt with no MSG
- ground black pepper to taste
- garlic powder to taste
- 2 tbsp butter
- 4 tbsp all-purpose flour, divided
- 1 lb. large shrimp, peeled and deveined
- 1 1/2 C. chicken stock
- 1 green onion, chopped

Directions

- Heat a large skillet on medium heat and cook the bacon till browned completely.
- Transfer the bacon onto a paper towel lined plate to drain and then crumble it.
- In the same skillet, melt the butter with the bacon grease.
- Sprinkle 3 tbsp of the flour on to and immediately, reduce the heat to medium-low.
- Cook for about 12 minutes, stirring continuously.

- Increase the heat to medium-high and sauté the onions and bell pepper for about 2 minutes.
- Meanwhile in a bowl, add the shrimp, seasoned salt, pepper, garlic powder and remaining flour and toss to coat well.
- Add the shrimp into the skillet and cook for about 1 minute, stirring continuously. s
- Add the chicken stock and stir to combine well.
- Reduce the heat to low and simmer for just a few minutes.
- Sprinkle with the green onion and remove from the heat.
- Serve with a toping of the bacon.

Amount per serving (4 total)

Timing Information:

Preparation	20 m
Cooking	20 m
Total Time	40 m

Nutritional Information:

Calories	263 kcal
Fat	11.1 g
Carbohydrates	12.6g
Protein	27.5 g
Cholesterol	196 mg
Sodium	1088 mg

* Percent Daily Values are based on a 2,000 calorie diet.

Southern Mountain Salad

Ingredients

- 4 slices bacon
- 4 green onions, chopped
- 1 head leaf lettuce - rinsed, dried and torn into bite-size pieces

Directions

- Heat a large skillet on medium-high heat and cook the bacon for about 10 minutes, turning occasionally.
- Transfer the bacon onto a paper towel lined plate to drain and then crumble it.
- In the same skillet, add the green onions and sauté for about 1 minute.
- In a serving bowl, place the lettuce.
- Place the green onions with bacon grease and gently, toss to coat.
- Serve immediately with a toping of the bacon.

Amount per serving (4 total)

Timing Information:

Preparation	10 m
Cooking	10 m
Total Time	20 m

Nutritional Information:

Calories	144 kcal
Fat	12.7 g
Carbohydrates	3.2g
Protein	4.5 g
Cholesterol	19 mg
Sodium	255 mg

* Percent Daily Values are based on a 2,000 calorie diet.

HOW TO MAKE GRITS

Ingredients

- 3 C. shrimp stock, divided
- 1 C. finely ground cornmeal
- 1 tbsp butter
- 1/2 C. shredded sharp Cheddar cheese
- salt and ground black pepper to taste
- 2 tbsp canola oil
- 1/2 C. diced celery
- 1 C. diced onion
- 1 C. diced green bell pepper
- 1 tbsp dried thyme
- 1 tbsp dried oregano
- 1 (8 oz.) can tomato sauce
- 1/3 C. reduced-fat sour cream
- 1 1/2 lb. uncooked shrimp, peeled and deveined
- 1 dash hot pepper sauce
- 1 tsp chopped green onion

Directions

- In a pan, add 2 C. of the shrimp stock and bring to a boil.
- Reduce the heat to low and let the stock simmer.

- In a bowl, add the cornmeal and remaining 1 C. of the shrimp stock and beat till smooth.
- Slowly, add the cornmeal mixture into the simmering shrimp stock, beating continuously.
- Cook for about 3-5 minutes, stirring occasionally.
- Stir in the butter till well combined.
- Slowly, add the Cheddar cheese, 1 tbsp at a time and stir till the cheese melts completely.
- Again, bring to a simmer and cook for about 15-20 minutes, stirring occasionally.
- Stir in the salt and black pepper.
- Meanwhile in a large skillet, heat the canola oil on medium heat and sauté the celery for about 3-4 minutes.
- Stir in the onion, green bell pepper, thyme and oregano and cook for about 7-8 minutes.
- Stir in the tomato sauce and simmer for about 5 minutes.
- Add the sour cream and stir to combine.
- Stir in the shrimp and bring to a gentle boil.
- Reduce the heat to low and simmer for about 5-7 minutes.
- Transfer the grits into a large shallow serving bowl and top with the shrimp.
- Place the vegetables mixture over the shrimp and grits and drizzle with the hot pepper sauce.
- Serve with a garnishing of the green onion.

Amount per serving (6 total)

Timing Information:

Preparation	20 m
Cooking	40 m
Total Time	1 h

Nutritional Information:

Calories	336 kcal
Fat	13.7 g
Carbohydrates	26.3g
Protein	26.5 g
Cholesterol	193 mg
Sodium	865 mg

* Percent Daily Values are based on a 2,000 calorie diet.

Rocky Mount Rice

Ingredients

- 2 C. uncooked long-grain white rice
- 6 C. boiling water
- 1 tbsp salt
- 6 slices bacon
- 2 onions, chopped
- 1 (8 oz.) can tomato sauce
- 1 (6 oz.) can tomato paste
- 1 tbsp white sugar
- 2 tsp Worcestershire sauce
- 1 dash hot pepper sauce

Directions

- Set your oven to 325 degrees F before doing anything else and grease a 2-quart baking dish.
- In a pan, add the rice, water and salt and bring to a boil.
- Reduce the heat to medium-low and simmer, covered for about 20-25 minutes.
- Meanwhile, heat a large skillet on medium-high heat and cook the bacon for about 10 minutes, turning occasionally.

- Transfer the bacon onto a paper towel lined plate to drain and then crumble it.
- Drain the grease, reserving about 1 tbsp in the skillet and reduce the heat to medium.
- In the same skillet, cook the onions for about 5-8 minutes.
- Stir in the crumbled bacon, tomato sauce, tomato paste, sugar, Worcestershire sauce and hot sauce and bring to a gentle boil.
- Reduce the heat and simmer for about 10 minutes.
- Place the cooked rice and bacon mixture into the prepared baking dish and stir to combine.
- Cover the dish and cook in the oven for about 45 minutes.

Amount per serving (8 total)

Timing Information:

Preparation	15 m
Cooking	1 h 5 m
Total Time	1 h 20 m

Nutritional Information:

Calories	331 kcal
Fat	10.1 g
Carbohydrates	51.9g
Protein	8.1 g
Cholesterol	14 mg
Sodium	1388 mg

* Percent Daily Values are based on a 2,000 calorie diet.

CHARLESTON CHILI

Ingredients

- 2 1/2 lb. ground beef
- 3 tbsp olive oil
- 3 stalks celery, diced
- 2 large onions, diced
- 2 cloves garlic, minced
- 1 (29 oz.) can tomato sauce
- 1 (28 oz.) can crushed tomatoes
- 1 (6 oz.) can mushrooms, drained
- 1 1/2 C. dark beer
- 2 (16 oz.) cans chili beans, drained
- 1 (15 oz.) can kidney beans, drained
- 1 tbsp ground cumin
- 1/4 C. chili powder
- 2 tsp ground coriander
- 2 tsp cayenne pepper
- 1 dash Worcestershire sauce

Directions

- Heat a large skillet on medium heat and cook the beef till browned completely.

- Drain the excess grease from the skillet.
- In a large pan, heat the oil on medium heat and sauté the celery, onions and garlic till the onion becomes translucent.
- Stir in the coked beef and remaining ingredients and bring to a gentle simmer.
- Reduce the heat to low and simmer for about 3 hours.

Amount per serving (12 total)

Timing Information:

Preparation	15 m
Cooking	3 h 20 m
Total Time	3 h 35 m

Nutritional Information:

Calories	389 kcal
Fat	18.1 g
Carbohydrates	34g
Protein	25.7 g
Cholesterol	57 mg
Sodium	1001 mg

* Percent Daily Values are based on a 2,000 calorie diet.

DURHAM BURGERS

Ingredients

- 1 lb. ground beef (lean)
- 1/4 C. packed brown sugar
- 1/4 C. beer, optional
- 1/4 C. yellow mustard
- 1/4 C. cider vinegar
- 1 C. thinly sliced cabbage
- 4 hamburger buns, split and toasted

Directions

- For the barbecue sauce in a small bowl, mix together the brown sugar, beer, mustard and vinegar and bring to a boil.
- Reduce the heat and simmer for about 15-17 minutes, stirring occasionally.
- Set your gas grill for medium heat and lightly, grease the grill grate.
- Make 4 (1/2-inch thick) patties from the ground beef.
- Arrange the patties onto the grill and cook, covered for about 7-9 minutes, flipping occasionally.
- In the last 2 minutes of the cooking, place the bun onto the grill, cut sides down and cook till toasted slightly.

- Spread about 1 tbsp of the sauce over bottom of each bun and top with 1 patty, followed by the cabbage and remaining sauce.
- Cover with the top bun and serve.

Amount per serving (4 total)

Timing Information:

Preparation	
Cooking	
Total Time	25 m

Nutritional Information:

Calories	400 kcal
Fat	15.6 g
Carbohydrates	37.7g
Protein	24.5 g
Cholesterol	66 mg
Sodium	481 mg

* Percent Daily Values are based on a 2,000 calorie diet.

Fried Chicken South Carolina Style

Ingredients

- 1 quart whole milk
- kosher salt
- 1/2 C. sugar
- 2 (4 lb) roasting chickens, each cut into 8 pieces
- 2 C. buttermilk
- 2 large eggs, lightly beaten
- 1 tsp sweet paprika
- 1 tsp hot sauce
- 1/2 tsp fresh ground pepper
- 2 tsp baking powder
- 1 1/2 tsp baking soda
- 5 C. all-purpose flour
- vegetable oil, for frying

Directions

- In a small pan, mix together 1 C. of the milk, 3/4 C. of the kosher salt and sugar on medium heat and cook for about 2 minutes, stirring continuously.
- Transfer the mixture into a large, deep bowl.

- Add the remaining 3 C. of the milk and chicken pieces and stir to combine.
- Refrigerate for about 4 hours.
- Drain the chicken and rinse under the cold running water.
- With the paper towels, pat dry the chicken pieces completely.
- In a bowl, add the buttermilk, eggs, 1 tbsp of the kosher salt, paprika, hot sauce, pepper, baking powder and baking soda and mix till well combined.
- In a large bowl, place the flour.
- Coat the chicken pieces with the flour, tapping off any excess.
- Dip the chicken pieces in the buttermilk mixture, letting the excess drip off.
- Place the chicken pieces into the bowl of the flour and turn to coat.
- In a large, deep skillet, heat the oil on medium heat and cook the chicken pieces, covered for about 5 minutes.
- Uncover and cook for about 18-20 minutes, flipping occasionally.
- Transfer the chicken pieces onto the paper towel lined plate to drain.
- Serve hot or warm.

Servings Per Recipe: 6

Timing Information:

Preparation	1 hr
Total Time	1 hr

Nutritional Information:

Calories	1445.6
Fat	70.5g
Cholesterol	366.7mg
Sodium	903.9mg
Carbohydrates	108.7g
Protein	87.7g

* Percent Daily Values are based on a 2,000 calorie diet.

BBQ Chicken Southern Style

Ingredients

- 3/4 C. molasses
- 1/2 C. pure olive oil
- 1/2 C. ruby port
- 2 tbsp Dijon mustard
- 2 tbsp soy sauce
- 2 tbsp fresh ground pepper
- 1 tbsp Worcestershire sauce
- 1 shallot, minced
- 1 green onion, chopped
- 3 lbs chicken breasts, thighs, quarters, drumsticks, bone in

BBQ Sauce:

- 2 C. yellow mustard
- 3/4 C. light brown sugar
- 1/4 C. strong brewed coffee
- 2 tbsp honey
- 1 tbsp molasses
- 1 tbsp liquid smoke
- 2 tsp Worcestershire sauce
- 2 tsp Tabasco sauce

Directions

- For the sauce in a medium pan, mix together all the ingredients and bring to a gentle boil.
- Stir well and remove from the heat.
- Keep aside in the room temperature to cool.
- After cooling, transfer into a glass jar with lid and refrigerate.
- For the chicken in a large bowl, add all the ingredients except chicken and mix well.
- Keep aside in the room temperature for about 30 minutes.
- Add the chicken pieces and coat with the mixture generously.
- Refrigerate for overnight.
- Set the broiler of your oven and arrange oven rack about 12-inch from the heating element.
- Remove the chicken from the marinade and arrange the pieces onto a large baking sheet.
- coat the chicken pieces with the barbecue sauce and cook under the broiler for about 8-10 minutes per side, flipping occasionally and rotating.

Servings Per Recipe: 8

Timing Information:

Preparation	15 mins
Total Time	35 mins

Nutritional Information:

Calories	655.9
Fat	30.1g
Cholesterol	108.9mg
Sodium	693.8mg
Carbohydrates	56.3g
Protein	37.2g

* Percent Daily Values are based on a 2,000 calorie diet.

Fayetteville Hot Dogs

Ingredients

- 8 hot dogs
- 8 hot dog buns
- 1 1/4 lbs extra lean ground beef
- 1 C. chopped onion
- 1 (6 oz.) cans tomato paste
- 1/2 C. ketchup
- 1 tbsp chili powder
- 2 tsp Worcestershire sauce
- 1 tsp cider vinegar
- 1 tsp salt
- 1/4 tsp black pepper

Directions

- In a 4 1/2-quart Dutch oven, add the beef and 2 C. of the water on high heat and bring to a boil.
- Add the onion and again bring to a boil.
- Reduce the heat to medium and stir to break the beef.
- Add the tomato paste, ketchup, chili powder, Worcestershire sauce, vinegar, salt, and pepper and stir till the tomato paste dissolves completely.

- Reduce the heat to medium-low and simmer for about 15 minutes, stirring after every 5 minutes.
- Meanwhile, set your gas grill to medium-high heat.
- Cook the hot dogs on the grill for about 5 minutes.
- Arrange each hot dog in a bun and top with the chili.
- Serve immediately.

Servings Per Recipe: 8

Timing Information:

Preparation	10 mins
Total Time	40 mins

Nutritional Information:

Calories	409.6
Fat	19.0g
Cholesterol	67.7mg
Sodium	1423.9mg
Carbohydrates	33.5g
Protein	25.8g

* Percent Daily Values are based on a 2,000 calorie diet.

GRANDMA'S BAKED CHICKEN

Ingredients

- 1 (3 1/2-4 lb) broiler-fryer chickens
- 1 sweet onion, cut into large chunks
- 1 small apple, unpeeled and cut into large chunks
- 2 small celery ribs
- fresh herb
- salt
- freshly grated black pepper

Glaze:

- 1 tbsp oil
- 2 tbsp apple juice
- 2 tbsp honey
- 1 tbsp lime juice
- 1/2 tsp paprika
- 1/4 tsp sea salt

Directions

- Set your oven to 325 degrees F before doing anything else and arrange a rack in a large roasting pan.
- Wash the chicken and with the paper towels, pat dry.
- Season the cavity of the chicken with the salt and pepper.

- Stuff the cavity with the onion, apple and celery and with the cooking string, tie the legs.
- For the glaze in a small bowl, mix together all the ingredients.
- Rub the whole chicken with a small amount of the glaze evenly.
- Reserve the remaining glaze.
- Arrange the chicken over the rack in roasting pan and cook in the oven for about 2 hours, basting with the glaze and pan juices after every 20-30 minutes.
- Remove from the oven and with a piece of the foil, cover the chicken and keep aside for about 10-15 minutes before carving.

Servings Per Recipe: 4

Timing Information:

| Preparation | 0 mins |
| Total Time | 1 hr 15 mins |

Nutritional Information:

Calories	944.3
Fat	63.3g
Cholesterol	297.9mg
Sodium	431.8mg
Carbohydrates	15.8g
Protein	74.3g

* Percent Daily Values are based on a 2,000 calorie diet.

Wake Forest Chili

Ingredients

- 1 lb ground beef
- 1 small onion, chopped
- 2 garlic cloves, finely minced
- 1 jalapeño pepper, chopped
- 1 (28 oz.) cans crushed tomatoes
- 2 (15 oz.) cans red kidney beans
- 1 (6 oz.) cans tomato paste
- 1 C. water
- 1 tsp salt
- 1 tbsp chili powder
- 1 tbsp ground cayenne pepper
- 1 tsp oregano
- 1 tsp paprika
- 1 tsp cumin
- 1/2 tsp dry mustard
- 1/4 tsp white pepper
- 1/2 tsp black pepper
- 1 bay leaf

Directions

- Heat a skillet and cook the beef, onions, garlic and jalapeño pepper till browned completely.
- Drain the excess grease from the skillet.
- Transfer the beef mixture into a crock pot.
- Add the remaining ingredients and stir to combine.
- Set the crock pot on Low and cook, covered for about 6 hours.

Servings Per Recipe: 6

Timing Information:

Preparation	15 mins
Total Time	6 hrs 15 mins

Nutritional Information:

Calories	418.3
Fat	13.0g
Cholesterol	51.4mg
Sodium	964.6mg
Carbohydrates	49.4g
Protein	29.2g

* Percent Daily Values are based on a 2,000 calorie diet.

Carolina Backyard Stuffing

Ingredients

- 6 C. cornbread (cooked and crumbled)
- saltine crackers, 1 sleeve, crushed
- 2 C. bread, toasted and crumbled
- 1/2 C. diced onion
- 1/2 C. celery, diced
- 1 (10 1/2 oz.) cans cream of mushroom soup
- 1 roll of pork sausage, sage
- 4 -5 C. chicken broth
- 2 eggs
- 1 -2 tbsp poultry seasoning
- 2 tbsp butter
- salt and pepper

Directions

- Set your oven to 350 degrees F before doing anything else and grease a baking dish.
- In a pan, melt the butter and sauté the onions and celery till translucent.
- Stir in the sausage and cook till cooked through.
- In a large bowl, mix together the cornbread, crushed saltine crackers and bread cubes.

- Add the sausage mixture and mix.
- In another bowl, mix together the chicken broth and eggs.
- Add the egg mixture, can of soup, poultry seasoning, salt and pepper into bread mixture and mix till well combined.
- Place the mixture into the prepared baking dish evenly.
- Cook in the oven for about 45-60 minutes.

Servings Per Recipe: 6

Timing Information:

| Preparation | 30 mins |
| Total Time | 1 hr 15 mins |

Nutritional Information:

Calories	174.8
Fat	9.8g
Cholesterol	72.1mg
Sodium	987.6mg
Carbohydrates	13.6g
Protein	7.6g

* Percent Daily Values are based on a 2,000 calorie diet.

Gardner's Casserole

Ingredients

- 3 packages frozen white corn in butter sauce
- 8 oz. sour cream
- 1 small chopped onion
- 1 can cream of celery soup
- 1 package sliced almonds
- 1/2 C. butter
- 1 package of crushed Ritz cracker

Directions

- Set your oven to 350 degrees F before doing anything else.
- In a pan, melt butter and sauté the almonds till desired doneness.
- In a bowl, mix together the white corn, sour cream, onion and celery soup.
- In the bottom of a casserole dish, place the corn mixture evenly.
- Spread the crackers over the corn mixture evenly and top with the almond sauté.
- Cook in the oven for about 45 minutes.

Servings Per Recipe: 8

Timing Information:

| Preparation | 5 mins |
| Total Time | 1 hr 5 mins |

Nutritional Information:

Calories	196.8
Fat	19.4g
Cholesterol	47.8mg
Sodium	386.4mg
Carbohydrates	4.8g
Protein	1.6g

* Percent Daily Values are based on a 2,000 calorie diet.

CHICKEN AND RICE CAROLINA STYLE

Ingredients

- 12 oz. bacon, chopped
- 2 C. long-grain rice
- 4 C. chicken broth, boiling
- 1 whole chicken, cut up (3 1/2 lb.)
- 4 stalks celery, cut into 1 inch pieces
- 1 carrot, cut in 1 inch pieces
- 1 bay leaf
- salt and pepper
- 2 tbsp fresh parsley, chopped

Directions

- Heat a large skillet and cook the bacon on very low heat till crisp.
- Transfer the bacon onto a paper towel lined plate to drain and then crumble it.
- Drain the grease, leaving 2 tbsp inside the skillet.
- In the same skillet, add the rice and cook slowly till browned lightly.
- Stir in the boiling stock and bring back to a boil.
- Stir in the chicken, vegetables, bay leaf, salt and pepper.

- Reduce the heat and simmer, covered for about 30 minutes.
- Serve hot with a sprinkling of the crumbled bacon and parsley.

Servings Per Recipe: 10

Timing Information:

Preparation	10 mins
Total Time	50 mins

Nutritional Information:

Calories	509.6
Fat	30.0g
Cholesterol	92.1mg
Sodium	665.7mg
Carbohydrates	31.2g
Protein	25.8g

* Percent Daily Values are based on a 2,000 calorie diet.

CHICKEN WINGS AND HOT SAUCE

Ingredients

- 1 gallon peanut oil
- 25 chicken wings, segmented and patted dry with paper towels
- 1/3 C. unsalted butter, melted
- 1/2 C. hot pepper sauce
- 1 tbsp garlic powder
- 1 tbsp coarse-ground black pepper

Directions

- In a deep-fryer, heat the oil to 375 degrees F.
- Gently add the wings, one at a time, to the hot oil and gently fry for about 15 minutes.
- In a large bowl, add the the melted butter, hot pepper sauce, garlic powder and black pepper and mix till well combined.
- Add the cooked wings and turn to coat.
- Serve immediately.

Amount per serving (4 total)

Timing Information:

Preparation	30 m
Cooking	15 m
Total Time	45 m

Nutritional Information:

Calories	1231 kcal
Fat	116.7 g
Carbohydrates	3.1g
Protein	44.2 g
Cholesterol	161 mg
Sodium	980 mg

* Percent Daily Values are based on a 2,000 calorie diet.

CAROLINA MACKEREL

Ingredients

- 1 (15 oz.) can mackerel, undrained
- 1 (10.75 oz.) can tomato soup
- 4 potatoes, sliced
- 1 onion, sliced
- red pepper flakes (to taste)
- 1 egg

Directions

- In a medium pan, add the undrained mackerel, tomato soup, potatoes, onion and red pepper flakes and enough water to cover on medium-high heat and bring to a boil.
- Reduce the heat and simmer for about 30 minutes.
- Break the egg over the hot stew and serve.

Amount per serving (4 total)

Timing Information:

Preparation	15 m
Cooking	30 m
Total Time	45 m

Nutritional Information:

Calories	339 kcal
Fat	7.3 g
Carbohydrates	40.9g
Protein	27.2 g
Cholesterol	118 mg
Sodium	394 mg

* Percent Daily Values are based on a 2,000 calorie diet.

Sour Salmon

Ingredients

- 4 (6 oz.) thick salmon fillets
- 1 (6 oz.) can lump crabmeat, divided
- 4 slices smoked Gouda cheese
- 1/4 C. butter, melted
- 2 lemons, juiced - divided
- 1 (8 oz.) carton sour cream
- 1 tbsp finely chopped fresh dill
- 1 (2 oz.) jar capers in brine, drained

Directions

- Set your oven to 350 degrees F before doing anything else.
- Trim the salmon fillets to remove thin portion.
- With a very sharp knife, cut the salmon fillets horizontally through the center but leave one end uncut so the fillet opens like a book.
- Place 1/4 of the lump crab meat over each opened fillet and top with a smoked Gouda slice.
- Close the fillets.
- In a small bowl, mix together the melted butter and juice of 1 lemon.

- Arrange each fillet into a single-serving baking dish and drizzle the lemon butter evenly.
- Cook in the oven for about 30 minutes.
- In a bowl, mix together the juice of the 2nd lemon, sour cream and dill.
- Spread the sour cream mixture over each baked fillet evenly.
- Serve immediately with a sprinkling of the capers.

Amount per serving (4 total)

Timing Information:

Preparation	20 m
Cooking	30 m
Total Time	50 m

Nutritional Information:

Calories	607 kcal
Fat	42.5 g
Carbohydrates	5.7g
Protein	49.8 g
Cholesterol	207 mg
Sodium	965 mg

* Percent Daily Values are based on a 2,000 calorie diet.

How to Make a Steak Durham Style

Ingredients

- 4 lb. trimmed skirt steaks
- 2 C. olive oil
- 1 C. red wine
- 2 tbsp dried parsley
- 2 tbsp dried basil
- 2 tbsp balsamic vinegar
- 2 tbsp soy sauce
- 6 cloves garlic, crushed
- 2 bay leaves
- 2 C. barbecue sauce

Directions

- With a sharp knife, make 1/4-1/2-inch diagonal cuts through the skirt steak on both sides.
- Then cut diagonally in the opposite, perpendicular direction.
- In a large glass bowl, add the olive oil, red wine, parsley, basil, balsamic vinegar, soy sauce, garlic and bay leaves and beat till well combined.
- Add the skirt steaks and toss to coat evenly.

- With a plastic wrap, cover the bowl and refrigerator for at least 8 hours to overnight.
- Set your outdoor grill for medium heat and lightly, grease the grill grate.
- Remove the skirt steaks from the bowl and shake off excess marinade.
- Discard the remaining marinade.
- Cook the skirt steak on the grill for about 10 minutes per side.
- Now, coat the steaks with the barbecue sauce and cook for about 2 minutes.
- Flip the side of the steaks and coat with the barbecue sauce and cook for about 2 minutes.

Amount per serving (16 total)

Timing Information:

Preparation	20 m
Cooking	25 m
Total Time	8 h 45 m

Nutritional Information:

Calories	404 kcal
Fat	31.7 g
Carbohydrates	12.8g
Protein	14 g
Cholesterol	25 mg
Sodium	491 mg

* Percent Daily Values are based on a 2,000 calorie diet.

Buttery Bush Mushrooms

Ingredients

- 6 tbsp butter
- 2 lb. medium fresh mushrooms, stems removed
- 1 (8 oz.) package Neufchatel cheese
- 1 (4 oz.) package goat cheese crumbles
- 2 tbsp finely chopped onion
- 1/2 C. mushroom stems, chopped
- 1/4 C. butter
- 1 tbsp finely chopped garlic

Directions

- In a large skillet, melt 3 tbsp of the butter on medium-high heat and cook half of the mushroom caps for about 5 minutes.
- Transfer the mushrooms in a colander to drain.
- repeat with the remaining butter and mushrooms.
- Transfer the mushrooms in the same colander and keep aside to cool.
- In a bowl, add the cream cheese and goat cheese and mix till well combined.
- Add the onions and mushroom stems and mix well.

- Fill each mushroom cap with the cheese mixture generously.
- Arrange the mushroom caps into a baking dish, filling side up.
- Set the broiler of your oven for high heat.
- In a small pan, melt remaining 1/4 C. of the butter with the garlic on medium heat and then sauté for about 1 minute.
- Drizzle the garlic butter over the filled mushroom caps.
- Cook in the oven for about 5 minutes.

Amount per serving (6 total)

Timing Information:

Preparation	30 m
Cooking	15 m
Total Time	45 m

Nutritional Information:

Calories	373 kcal
Fat	34.1 g
Carbohydrates	7.5g
Protein	13 g
Cholesterol	94 mg
Sodium	391 mg

* Percent Daily Values are based on a 2,000 calorie diet.

Carolina Kitchen Mushrooms

Ingredients

- 4 Portobello mushrooms
- 1 large onion, sliced 1/4 inch thick
- 1/4 C. balsamic vinegar
- 1 eggplant, sliced into 1/2 inch rounds
- 1 tomato, sliced 1/2 inch thick
- 4 slices provolone cheese

Directions

- In a bowl, mix together the the mushrooms, onions and balsamic vinegar and keep aside for about 20 minutes.
- Set your oven to 350 degrees F.
- In the bottom of a non-stick baking dish, place the eggplant, followed by the mushroom, onion, tomato and cheese.
- Cook in the oven for about 30 minutes.

Amount per serving (4 total)

Timing Information:

Preparation	20 m
Cooking	30 m
Total Time	50 m

Nutritional Information:

Calories	195 kcal
Fat	8.2 g
Carbohydrates	21.5g
Protein	12.2 g
Cholesterol	20 mg
Sodium	267 mg

* Percent Daily Values are based on a 2,000 calorie diet.

DEEP SOUTH CHOWDER

Ingredients

- 1 tbsp vegetable oil
- 1 large onion, chopped
- 5 stalks celery, sliced
- 4 carrots, sliced
- 4 C. peeled, cubed white potatoes
- 2 (16 oz.) cans minced clams, with juice
- 3 quarts clam juice
- 1 tsp dried thyme
- 1/2 tsp ground black pepper
- 8 slices crisp cooked bacon, crumbled

Directions

- In a large pan, heat the oil on medium heat and sauté the onion, celery and carrots till tender.
- Stir in the potatoes, clams, clam juice, thyme, pepper and bacon and bring to a boil.
- Reduce the heat and simmer for about 20 minutes.

Amount per serving (8 total)

Timing Information:

Preparation	20 m
Cooking	30 m
Total Time	50 m

Nutritional Information:

Calories	297 kcal
Fat	6.7 g
Carbohydrates	23.8g
Protein	34.3 g
Cholesterol	92 mg
Sodium	1079 mg

* Percent Daily Values are based on a 2,000 calorie diet.

American Burgers

Ingredients

- 2 lb. ground beef sirloin
- 1/2 onion, grated
- 1 tbsp grill seasoning
- 1 tbsp liquid smoke flavoring
- 2 tbsp Worcestershire sauce
- 2 tbsp minced garlic
- 1 tbsp adobo sauce from canned chipotle peppers
- 1 chipotle chile in adobo sauce, chopped
- salt and pepper to taste
- 6 (1 oz.) slices sharp Cheddar cheese
- 6 hamburger buns

Directions

- Set your grill for medium-high heat and lightly, grease the grill grate.
- In a large bowl, add the ground sirloin, onion, grill seasoning, liquid smoke, Worcestershire sauce, garlic, adobo sauce, chipotle pepper, salt and pepper and mix till well combined.
- Make 6 equal sized patties from the mixture.
- Cook the patties on the grill till done completely.

- In the last 1 minute of cooking, place 1 Cheddar cheese slice over each patty.
- Arrange 1 patty over each bun and serve.

Amount per serving (6 total)

Timing Information:

Preparation	25 m
Cooking	10 m
Total Time	35 m

Nutritional Information:

Calories	537 kcal
Fat	29.7 g
Carbohydrates	26.6g
Protein	38.7 g
Cholesterol	121 mg
Sodium	1035 mg

* Percent Daily Values are based on a 2,000 calorie diet.

SOUTH CAROLINA HUMMUS

Ingredients

- 3 tbsp safflower oil
- 2 tbsp tahini
- 2 tbsp fresh lemon juice
- 1 tbsp white vinegar
- 1 1/2 tsp tamari
- 1/2 tsp ground cumin
- 1/2 tsp Celtic sea salt
- 1/2 tsp ground black pepper
- 1 clove garlic, minced
- 1 (1x4 inch) piece kombu seaweed
- 1 pinch cayenne pepper
- 1 3/4 C. cooked lima beans
- 1 tbsp chopped fresh parsley

Directions

- In a food processor, add the safflower oil, tahini, lemon juice, vinegar, tamari, cumin, salt, black pepper, garlic, kombu and cayenne pepper and pulse till smooth.
- Add the lima beans and pulse till smooth.
- Add the parsley and pulse till just combined.

Amount per serving (6 total)

Timing Information:

Preparation	
Cooking	10 m
Total Time	10 m

Nutritional Information:

Calories	204 kcal
Fat	9.7 g
Carbohydrates	23.3g
Protein	6.8 g
Cholesterol	0 mg
Sodium	1035 mg

* Percent Daily Values are based on a 2,000 calorie diet.

BANANA PEANUT BUTTER LUNCH BOX SANDWICH

Ingredients

- cooking spray
- 2 tbsp peanut butter
- 2 slices whole wheat bread
- 1 banana, sliced

Directions

- Spread 1 tbsp of the peanut butter over one side of each bread slice.
- Arrange the banana slices over the buttered side of 1 slice and top with the other slice, buttered side down.
- With the back of the spatula, press the sandwich firmly.
- Grease a skillet with the cooking spray and heat on medium heat.
- Cook the sandwich for about 2 minutes per side.

Amount per serving (1 total)

Timing Information:

Preparation	2 m
Cooking	10 m
Total Time	12 m

Nutritional Information:

Calories	437 kcal
Fat	18.7 g
Carbohydrates	56.8g
Protein	16.8 g
Cholesterol	0 mg
Sodium	422 mg

* Percent Daily Values are based on a 2,000 calorie diet.

NORTH CAROLINA MOON PIES

Ingredients

- 1/2 C. butter, softened
- 1 C. white sugar
- 1 egg
- 1 C. evaporated milk
- 1 tsp vanilla extract
- 2 C. all-purpose flour
- 1/2 tsp salt
- 1/2 C. unsweetened cocoa powder
- 1 1/2 tsp baking soda
- 1/2 tsp baking powder
- 1/2 C. butter, softened
- 1 C. confectioners' sugar
- 1/2 tsp vanilla extract
- 1 C. marshmallow creme

Directions

- Set your oven to 400 degrees F before doing anything else and lightly, grease a cookie sheet.
- For the cookie crusts in a large bowl, add 1/2 C. of the butter and white sugar and beat till creamy.

- Add the egg, evaporated milk and vanilla and mix till well combined.
- In another bowl, mix together the flour, salt, cocoa powder, baking soda and baking powder.
- Slowly, add the flour mixture into the sugar mixture and mix till just combined.
- With rounded tbsps, place the dough onto the prepared cookie sheet, about 3-inch apart.
- Cook in the oven for about 6-8 minutes.
- Remove from the oven and keep onto the wire rack to cool in the pan for about 5 minutes.
- Carefully, invert the cookies onto the wire rack to cool for at least 1 hour before filling.
- For the filling in a bowl, add 1/2 C. butter, confectioners' sugar, flavored extract and marshmallow crème and mix till smooth.
- Spread 1-2 tbsps of the filling over the flat side of a cookie crust and cover with the flat side of another cookie crust.
- Repeat with the remaining cookies.

Amount per serving (24 total)

Timing Information:

Preparation	30 m
Cooking	8 m
Total Time	38 m

Nutritional Information:

Calories	193 kcal
Fat	9 g
Carbohydrates	26.7g
Protein	2.5 g
Cholesterol	31 mg
Sodium	210 mg

* Percent Daily Values are based on a 2,000 calorie diet.

EMERALD ISLE CORNBREAD

Ingredients

- 1 C. cornmeal
- 1 C. all-purpose flour
- 1/2 C. white sugar
- 3 tsp baking powder
- 1 tsp salt
- 2 eggs
- 2/3 C. milk
- 1/2 C. vegetable oil
- 2 C. blueberries

Directions

- Set your oven to 350 degrees F before doing anything else and grease a 9-inch square baking dish.
- In a bowl, mix together the cornmeal, flour, sugar, baking powder and salt.
- In another bowl, add the eggs, milk and oil and beat till well combined.
- Add the cornmeal mixture and mix till just combined.
- Fold in the blueberries
- Place the mixture into the prepared baking dish evenly.

- Cook in the oven for about 25-30 minutes or till a toothpick inserted in the center comes out clean.

Amount per serving (6 total)

Timing Information:

Preparation	15 m
Cooking	25 m
Total Time	40 m

Nutritional Information:

Calories	453 kcal
Fat	21.3 g
Carbohydrates	59.8g
Protein	7.2 g
Cholesterol	64 mg
Sodium	668 mg

* Percent Daily Values are based on a 2,000 calorie diet.

SIMPLE BREAKFAST GRITS

Ingredients

- 1 quart water
- 1 tsp minced garlic
- 1 tsp salt
- 1 C. quick-cooking grits
- 1 1/2 C. diced processed cheese
- 1/4 C. butter
- 1 egg
- 1/4 C. milk

Directions

- Set your oven to 350 degrees F before doing anything else and grease a 2 quart casserole dish.
- In a large pan, add the water, garlic and salt and bring to a boil.
- Add the grits and stir to combine.
- Reduce the heat to low and simmer for about 5 minutes, stirring occasionally.
- Remove from the heat and stir in the cheese and butter till melted.
- In a small bowl, add the egg and milk and beat till well combined.

- Stir in the grits.
- Place the grits mixture in the prepared casserole dish evenly.
- Cook in the oven for about 20-25 minutes.

Amount per serving (5 total)

Timing Information:

Preparation	10 m
Cooking	25 m
Total Time	35 m

Nutritional Information:

Calories	378 kcal
Fat	24.2 g
Carbohydrates	26.5g
Protein	13.7 g
Cholesterol	93 mg
Sodium	1181 mg

* Percent Daily Values are based on a 2,000 calorie diet.

Hush Puppies

(Cornmeal Fritters)

Ingredients

- 6 C. all-purpose flour
- 3 C. cornmeal
- 1 C. white sugar
- 1 C. grated Parmesan cheese
- 1/4 C. baking powder
- salt and ground black pepper to taste
- 5 eggs
- 3 bell peppers, minced
- 3 onions, minced
- 1 (14 oz.) can cream-style corn
- 1 (14 oz.) can whole kernel corn
- 1 C. chopped pimento peppers
- 2 quarts vegetable oil for frying

Directions

- In a large bowl, add all the ingredients except the oil and mix till well combined.
- Make balls with 6-8 tbsp of the mixture.

- In a deep-fryer, heat the oil to 375 degrees F and fry the balls in batches for about 5 minutes.
- With a slotted spoon, transfer the hush puppies onto a paper towel lined plate to drain.

Amount per serving (24 total)

Timing Information:

Preparation	20 m
Cooking	10 m
Total Time	30 m

Nutritional Information:

Calories	348 kcal
Fat	10.3 g
Carbohydrates	56.8g
Protein	8.3 g
Cholesterol	42 mg
Sodium	411 mg

* Percent Daily Values are based on a 2,000 calorie diet.

REAL CAROLINA COLESLAW

Ingredients

- 1 (16 oz.) bag coleslaw mix
- 2 tbsp diced onion
- 2/3 C. creamy salad dressing
- 3 tbsp vegetable oil
- 1/2 C. white sugar
- 1 tbsp white vinegar
- 1/4 tsp salt
- 1/2 tsp poppy seeds

Directions

- In a large bowl, mix together the coleslaw mix and onion.
- In another bowl, add the salad dressing, vegetable oil, sugar, vinegar, salt and poppy seeds and beat till well combined.
- Place the dressing over the coleslaw mix and toss to coat well.
- Refrigerate to chill for at least 2 hours before serving.

Amount per serving (8 total)

Timing Information:

Preparation	
Cooking	15 m
Total Time	2 h 15 m

Nutritional Information:

Calories	200 kcal
Fat	12 g
Carbohydrates	22.5g
Protein	0.8 g
Cholesterol	11 mg
Sodium	253 mg

* Percent Daily Values are based on a 2,000 calorie diet.

Collard Greens from North Carolina

Ingredients

- 1 tbsp olive oil
- 3 slices bacon
- 1 large onion, chopped
- 2 cloves garlic, minced
- 1 tsp salt
- 1 tsp pepper
- 3 C. chicken broth
- 1 pinch red pepper flakes
- 1 lb. fresh collard greens, cut into 2-inch pieces

Directions

- In a large pan, heat the oil on medium-high heat and cook the bacon till crisp.
- Transfer the bacon onto a paper towel lined plate to drain and then crumble it.
- In the same pan, add the cooked bacon and onion and cook for about 5 minutes.
- Stir in the garlic and cook till just fragrant.
- Stir in the collard greens and stir fry till starts to wilt.

- Add the chicken broth, salt, pepper and red pepper flakes and stir to combine.
- Reduce heat to low and simmer, covered for about 45 minutes.

Amount per serving (6 total)

Timing Information:

Preparation	10 m
Cooking	1 h
Total Time	1 h 10 m

Nutritional Information:

Calories	127 kcal
Fat	9.2 g
Carbohydrates	7.9g
Protein	4.4 g
Cholesterol	12 mg
Sodium	1001 mg

* Percent Daily Values are based on a 2,000 calorie diet.

BBQ Rib Racks

Ingredients

- 1/2 C. brown sugar
- 1/3 C. fresh lemon juice
- 1/4 C. white vinegar
- 1/4 C. apple cider vinegar
- 1 tbsp Worcestershire sauce
- 1/4 C. molasses
- 2 C. prepared mustard
- 2 tsp dried minced garlic
- 2 tsp salt
- 1 tsp ground black pepper
- 1 tsp crushed red pepper flakes
- 1/2 tsp white pepper
- 1/4 tsp cayenne pepper
- 2 racks pork spareribs
- 1/2 C. barbecue seasoning

Directions

- Set your grill to 225-250 degrees F and lightly, grease the grill grate.

- In a bowl, add the brown sugar, lemon juice, white vinegar, cider vinegar, Worcestershire sauce, molasses, mustard, granulated garlic, salt, pepper, red pepper flakes, white pepper and cayenne pepper and mix till well combined.
- Coat the ribs with the barbecue seasoning generously.
- Place the ribs onto the grill and cook, covered for about 4 hours, basting with the sauce mixture generously during the last 30 minutes of the cooking.
- In a small pan, add the remaining sauce mixture and bring to a boil.
- Serve the ribs alongside the sauce.

Amount per serving (10 total)

Timing Information:

Preparation	30 m
Cooking	4 h
Total Time	4 h 30 m

Nutritional Information:

Calories	750 kcal
Fat	50.5 g
Carbohydrates	24g
Protein	48.8 g
Cholesterol	192 mg
Sodium	3406 mg

* Percent Daily Values are based on a 2,000 calorie diet.

Good Day Crab Boil

Ingredients

- 1 tbsp seafood seasoning
- 5 lb. new potatoes
- 3 (16 oz.) packages cooked kielbasa sausage, cut into 1 inch pieces
- 8 ears fresh corn, husks and silks removed
- 5 lb. whole crab, broken into pieces
- 4 lb. fresh shrimp, peeled and deveined

Directions

- Heat a large pan of water over an outdoor cooker.
- Stir in the Old Bay Seasoning and bring to a boil.
- Stir in the potatoes and sausage and cook for about 10 minutes.
- Stir in the corn and crab and cook for about 5 minutes.
- Stir in the shrimp and cook for about 3-4 minutes.
- Drain the liquid from the pan and serve.

Amount per serving (15 total)

Timing Information:

Preparation	30 m
Cooking	30 m
Total Time	1 h

Nutritional Information:

Calories	722 kcal
Fat	29.4 g
Carbohydrates	45.8g
Protein	67.6 g
Cholesterol	333 mg
Sodium	1576 mg

* Percent Daily Values are based on a 2,000 calorie diet.

YELLOW STONE GRITS

Ingredients

- 3/4 C. yellow stone-ground grits
- 3 C. milk
- 1/8 C. extra virgin olive oil
- 1 tsp butter
- 1 small onion, finely chopped
- 1 lb. shrimp, peeled and deveined
- 1/4 tsp salt
- 1/8 tsp white pepper

Directions

- In a medium pan, add the milk and bring to a boil.
- Add the grits and stir to combine.
- Reduce the heat to low and cook for about 10 minutes, stirring occasionally.
- Meanwhile in a skillet, heat the olive oil and butter on medium heat and sauté the onions till tender.
- Add the shrimp and toss too coat.
- Stir in the salt and pepper and cook for about 4-5 minutes.
- Add the shrimp mixture into the grits and stir to combine.
- Cook for about 10-15 minutes.

- Serve hot.

Amount per serving (4 total)

Timing Information:

Preparation	10 m
Cooking	30 m
Total Time	40 m

Nutritional Information:

Calories	387 kcal
Fat	13.6 g
Carbohydrates	33.3g
Protein	31.5 g
Cholesterol	190 mg
Sodium	396 mg

* Percent Daily Values are based on a 2,000 calorie diet.

SMOKED BEEF STEW

Ingredients

- 3 quarts water
- 1 lemon, halved
- 1 medium onion, halved
- 2 cloves garlic, crushed
- 1 pinch coarse salt
- 1 (3 oz.) package dry crab boil seasoning mix
- 1 1/2 lb. red potatoes, scrubbed
- 4 ears corn, husk and silk removed
- 1 1/2 lb. unpeeled, large fresh shrimp
- 1 lb. smoked beef sausage, cut into chunks
- 1/2 C. butter, melted
- 1 dash hot pepper sauce

Directions

- In a large pan of the boiling water, squeeze the juice from the lemon halves.
- Add the lemon halves, onion, garlic, salt and seasoning mix and stir to combine.
- Reduce the heat to medium-low and simmer, covered for about 10 minutes.
- Stir in the potatoes and sausage and bring to a boil.

- Simmer, covered for about 20 minutes.
- Break the ears of the corn in half and stir into the pan.
- Cook, covered for about 10 minutes.
- Remove from the heat and stir in the shrimp.
- Keep aside, covered for about 5 minutes.
- Drain the liquid from the pan.
- In a small bowl, mix together the melted butter and hot sauce.
- Serve the butter mixture alongside the stew.

Amount per serving (6 total)

Timing Information:

Preparation	10 m
Cooking	45 m
Total Time	55 m

Nutritional Information:

Calories	664 kcal
Fat	39 g
Carbohydrates	41.5g
Protein	39.4 g
Cholesterol	264 mg
Sodium	1237 mg

* Percent Daily Values are based on a 2,000 calorie diet.

LAKE LURE RED POTATO STEW

Ingredients

- 1 pound smoked sausage links, sliced
- 10 frozen small corn cobs
- 10 small red potatoes
- 1 (3 ounce) package dry crab boil seasoning mix
- 1 1/2 pounds unpeeled, large fresh shrimp
- salt to taste

Directions

- In a large pan, add the the sausage, corn, potatoes, seasoning mix and enough water to cover on high heat and bring to a boil.
- Reduce the heat to low and simmer for about 15 minutes.
- Stir in the shrimp and simmer for about 2-3 minutes.
- Drain the liquid from the skillet.
- Stir in the salt and serve hot.

Amount per serving (8 total)

Timing Information:

Preparation	15 m
Cooking	20 m
Total Time	35 m

Nutritional Information:

Calories	548 kcal
Fat	20.3 g
Carbohydrates	55g
Protein	34.2 g
Cholesterol	168 mg
Sodium	1303 mg

* Percent Daily Values are based on a 2,000 calorie diet.

SOUTH CAROLINA PIE

Ingredients

- 1 tbsp butter
- 1 C. chopped celery
- 1 C. chopped onion
- 1/2 C. chopped green pepper
- 1 (10 oz.) can refrigerated flaky biscuits
- 3 tomatoes, thinly sliced
- 1 C. shredded Cheddar cheese
- 1 C. low-fat mayonnaise
- 1 C. sour cream
- 1 tsp salt-free garlic and herb seasoning blend

Directions

- Set your oven to 350 degrees F before doing anything else and lightly, grease a medium baking dish.
- In a medium skillet, melt the butter on medium heat and sauté the celery, onion and green pepper till tender.
- In a bowl, mix together the Cheddar cheese, mayonnaise, sour cream, and salt-free seasoning blend.
- Place the biscuits in the prepared baking and press to make a smooth crust.

- Place the tomatoes over the crust evenly and top with the cooked vegetables.
- Place the cheese mixture over the vegetables evenly.
- Cook in the oven for about 45 minutes.
- Remove from the oven and keep aside to cool for about 15-20 minutes before serving.

Amount per serving (8 total)

Timing Information:

Preparation	15 m
Cooking	45 m
Total Time	1 h 15 m

Nutritional Information:

Calories	279 kcal
Fat	18.8 g
Carbohydrates	20g
Protein	8.5 g
Cholesterol	35 mg
Sodium	480 mg

* Percent Daily Values are based on a 2,000 calorie diet.

Annie's Grits

Ingredients

- 3/4 C. uncooked grits
- 6 oz. garlic flavored processed cheese, cubed
- 1 pinch cayenne pepper
- 2 tbsp butter
- 2 tbsp olive oil
- 2 cloves garlic, minced
- 1 tomato, diced
- 2 lb. fresh shrimp, peeled and deveined
- 1/2 lemon, juiced
- salt to taste

Directions

- Cook the grits according to package's directions.
- Stir in the cubed cheese and cayenne pepper and reduce the heat to low to keep the mixture warm.
- In a large skillet, heat the oil and butter on medium-high heat and sauté the garlic and tomato till the tomato begins to soften.
- Stir in the shrimp and lemon juice and cook till the shrimp are pink.
- Stir in the salt and remove from the heat.

- Place the warm grits onto a serving platter and top with the shrimp mixture.

Amount per serving (4 total)

Timing Information:

Preparation	20 m
Cooking	20 m
Total Time	40 m

Nutritional Information:

Calories	634 kcal
Fat	32.5 g
Carbohydrates	34.4g
Protein	50.4 g
Cholesterol	341 mg
Sodium	1054 mg

* Percent Daily Values are based on a 2,000 calorie diet.

Handmade Carolina Hot Sauce

Ingredients

- 1 lb. turkey bacon, diced
- 1 red onion, diced
- 1 tbsp minced garlic
- 1 bunch green onions, sliced
- 2 green bell peppers, chopped
- 2 yellow bell peppers chopped
- 8 jalapeño peppers, chopped
- 2 poblano peppers, chopped
- 1/2 C. sliced mushrooms
- 8 roma tomatoes, diced
- 2 (10 oz.) cans diced tomatoes with green chile peppers, drained
- 1 tsp lime juice
- 3/4 C. chopped cilantro
- 2 tsp salt
- 2 tsp black pepper

Directions

- Heat a large skillet on medium heat and cook the bacon till crisp.

- Remove the bacon, reserving 1 tbsp of the bacon grease in the skillet.
- In the same skillet, add the remaining ingredients and bring to a boil.
- Reduce the heat to medium-low and simmer till the desired consistency of the sauce is acquired.

Amount per serving (24 total)

Timing Information:

Preparation	50 m
Cooking	45 m
Total Time	1 h 35 m

Nutritional Information:

Calories	107 kcal
Fat	8.7 g
Carbohydrates	4.8g
Protein	3.2 g
Cholesterol	13 mg
Sodium	450 mg

* Percent Daily Values are based on a 2,000 calorie diet.

HOT DINNER BREAD

Ingredients

- 1 1/2 C. milk
- 4 tbsp butter
- 2 eggs, beaten
- 1/2 C. white sugar
- 1 tsp vanilla extract
- 4 C. bread flour
- 3 tsp active dry yeast
- 1 tsp salt
- 1/4 C. white sugar
- 1/4 C. brown sugar
- 1/3 C. bread flour
- 1/4 C. butter
- 1 egg
- 1 tbsp water

Directions

- In a small pan, add the milk and heat till it bubbles.
- Remove from the heat and stir in 4 tbsp of the butter till melted.
- Keep aside till the milk mixture becomes lukewarm.

- In a bread machine pan, add the milk mixture, 2 eggs, 1/2 C. of the sugar, vanilla extract, 4 C. of the bread flour, yeast and salt.
- Select the Dough setting and press Start.
- After the mixing is finished, leave the dough in the bread machine pan.
- With a towel, cover the pan for about 45 minutes.
- Transfer the dough onto a lightly floured surface and divide into 2 equal sized portions.
- Shape each dough portion into loaves.
- Arrange each bread loaf into 2 lightly greased 9x5-inch loaf pans.
- With the damp clothes, cover the bread loaves and keep aside for about 40 minutes.
- Set you oven to 350 degrees F.
- In a small bowl, mix together 1/4 C. of the sugar, 1/4 of the brown sugar and 1/3 C. of the flour.
- With a pastry blender, cut in the butter till a coarse crumbs like mixture forms.
- In another bowl, add 1 egg and 1 tbsp of the water and beat well.
- Coat the bread loaves with the egg wash and sprinkle with the crumb topping.
- Cook in the oven for about 30 minutes.

Amount per serving (20 total)

Timing Information:

Preparation	20 m
Cooking	30 m
Total Time	3 h

Nutritional Information:

Calories	206 kcal
Fat	6.2 g
Carbohydrates	32g
Protein	5.4 g
Cholesterol	42 mg
Sodium	168 mg

* Percent Daily Values are based on a 2,000 calorie diet.

PEANUT BUTTER BACON SANDWICH

Ingredients

- 3 tbsp peanut butter
- 2 slices white bread
- 1 banana, peeled and sliced
- 3 slices cooked turkey bacon
- 1 1/2 tsp butter

Directions

- Spread the peanut butter over 1 side of 1 bread slice evenly.
- Place the banana slices over the buttered slice of bread, followed by the bacon.
- Place the remaining bread slice on top to make a sandwich.
- Spread the butter over the outside of the sandwich evenly.
- Heat a skillet on medium heat and cook the sandwich for about 4 minutes per side.

Amount per serving (1 total)

Timing Information:

Preparation	10 m
Cooking	10 m
Total Time	20 m

Nutritional Information:

Calories	676 kcal
Fat	40.2 g
Carbohydrates	62.1g
Protein	24.1 g
Cholesterol	36 mg
Sodium	1025 mg

* Percent Daily Values are based on a 2,000 calorie diet.

BANANA MAYO SANDWICH

Ingredients

- 2 slices white bread
- 1 1/2 tbsp mayonnaise
- 1 banana, peeled and sliced

Directions

- Slice your banana into small pieces.
- Lay out your bread and coast each side evenly with the mayo.
- Place the banana one side of the bread and form a sandwich.

Amount per serving (1 total)

Timing Information:

Preparation	10 m
Cooking	0 m
Total Time	10 m

Nutritional Information:

Calories	476 kcal
Fat	30.2 g
Carbohydrates	52.1g
Protein	10.1 g
Cholesterol	36 mg
Sodium	1025 mg

* Percent Daily Values are based on a 2,000 calorie diet.

FANCY ZUCCHINI BAKE

Ingredients

- 1/2 C. shredded Swiss cheese
- 1 (9 inch) prepared pie crust
- 2 tsp olive oil
- 1 onion, minced
- 1 clove garlic, minced
- 2 zucchini, cut in half lengthwise, then cut into 1/2-inch half moons
- 6 tomatoes, cubed
- 1/2 tsp herbes de Provence
- salt and pepper to taste
- 2 eggs
- 1/4 C. milk

Directions

- Set your oven to 350 degrees F before doing anything else.
- In the bottom of the pie crust, spread the Swiss cheese and keep aside.
- In a large skillet, heat the oil on medium heat and sauté the onion and garlic for about 5 minutes.
- Stir in the zucchini, tomatoes, and herbes de Provence and cook for about 3 minutes.

- Stir in the salt and pepper.
- Reduce the heat to medium-low and cook, covered for about 20 minutes.
- Meanwhile in a small bowl, add the eggs and milk and beat till well combined.
- Place the vegetable mixture over the Swiss cheese in the pie crust evenly and with the back of the spoon, flatten the top surface.
- Spread the egg mixture on top evenly.
- Cook in the oven for about 20 minutes.

Amount per serving (6 total)

Timing Information:

Preparation	35 m
Cooking	50 m
Total Time	1 h 25 m

Nutritional Information:

Calories	270 kcal
Fat	16.3 g
Carbohydrates	23.8g
Protein	8.7 g
Cholesterol	71 mg
Sodium	213 mg

* Percent Daily Values are based on a 2,000 calorie diet.

HUSH PUPPIES II

Ingredients

- 1 C. self-rising flour
- 1 C. self-rising cornmeal
- 1/2 tsp garlic salt
- 1/2 tsp ground black pepper
- 1 (15 oz.) can cream-style corn
- 1/2 lb. crab meat
- 1 onion, diced
- 2 eggs, beaten
- 1 quart vegetable oil

Directions

- In a large bowl, add all the ingredients except the oil and mix till well combined.
- Keep aside for about 10 minutes.
- Make balls with 6-8 tbsp of the mixture.
- In a deep-fryer, heat the oil to 365 degrees F and fry the balls in batches for about 4-5 minutes.
- With a slotted spoon, transfer the hush puppies onto a paper towel lined plate to drain.

Amount per serving (8 total)

Timing Information:

Preparation	10 m
Cooking	10 m
Total Time	30 m

Nutritional Information:

Calories	329 kcal
Fat	13.7 g
Carbohydrates	40.6g
Protein	12.1 g
Cholesterol	68 mg
Sodium	935 mg

* Percent Daily Values are based on a 2,000 calorie diet.

ALTERNATIVE CAROLINA COLESLAW

Ingredients

- 2 C. chopped cabbage
- 4 kohlrabi bulbs, peeled and grated
- 2 stalks celery, sliced thin
- 2 carrots, sliced thin
- 2 tbsp minced fresh onion
- 1/3 C. white sugar
- 1/2 tsp salt
- 1/8 tsp ground black pepper
- 1/8 tsp celery seed
- 1/2 C. mayonnaise
- 4 1/2 tsp apple cider vinegar

Directions

- In a large bowl, add the cabbage, kohlrabi, celery, carrot and onion and toss to coat well.
- In another bowl, add the sugar, salt, pepper, celery seed, mayonnaise and vinegar and beat till smooth.
- Place the dressing over the cabbage mixture and stir to combine well.
- Refrigerate to chill for about 1 hour before serving.

Amount per serving (8 total)

Timing Information:

Preparation	
Cooking	25 m
Total Time	1 h 25 m

Nutritional Information:

Calories	173 kcal
Fat	11.1 g
Carbohydrates	18.3g
Protein	2.3 g
Cholesterol	5 mg
Sodium	267 mg

* Percent Daily Values are based on a 2,000 calorie diet.

Gardner's Inspired Greens

Ingredients

- 2 sweet onions, finely chopped
- 2 smoked ham hocks
- 4 cloves garlic, finely chopped
- 3 (32 oz.) containers chicken broth
- 3 (1 lb.) packages collard greens, trimmed
- 1/3 C. vinegar
- 2 tbsp white sugar
- 1 1/2 tsp salt
- 3/4 tsp ground black pepper

Directions

- In a large pan, add the onions, ham hocks, garlic and chicken broth on medium heat and cook for about 2 hours.
- Stir in the collard greens, vinegar, sugar, salt and pepper and cook for about 2 hours.

Amount per serving (10 total)

Timing Information:

Preparation	15 m
Cooking	4 h
Total Time	4 h 15 m

Nutritional Information:

Calories	187 kcal
Fat	9.7 g
Carbohydrates	14.1g
Protein	11.8 g
Cholesterol	34 mg
Sodium	1686 mg

* Percent Daily Values are based on a 2,000 calorie diet.

AMERICAN PINTO BEANS

Ingredients

- 6 1/4 C. water
- 1 C. condensed chicken broth
- 2 lb. dried pinto beans
- 5 cloves cloves garlic, chopped
- 1/2 red onion, chopped
- 1 tbsp red pepper flakes
- salt, to taste
- 1 (8 oz.) package shredded mozzarella cheese
- 1 (16 oz.) container pico de gallo, optional

Directions

- In a large pan, mix together the water, chicken broth, beans, garlic, onion, red pepper flakes, salt and pepper and bring to a gentle simmer.
- Simmer, covered for about 3 1/2 hours. (You can add extra water to keep the beans from drying out.)
- With a potato masher, mash the cooked beans till desired consistency is achieved.
- Stir in the mozzarella cheese and pico de gallo and serve immediately.

Amount per serving (16 total)

Timing Information:

Preparation	15 m
Cooking	4 h
Total Time	4 h 15 m

Nutritional Information:

Calories	252 kcal
Fat	3.2 g
Carbohydrates	38g
Protein	16.4 g
Cholesterol	9 mg
Sodium	328 mg

* Percent Daily Values are based on a 2,000 calorie diet.

BLACK EYED DINNER

Ingredients

- 1/3 C. vegetable oil
- 1/3 C. all-purpose flour
- 2 tbsp vegetable oil
- 1 1/2 C. chopped okra
- 1 C. chopped onion
- 3/4 C. chopped celery
- 3 cloves garlic, peeled and minced
- 4 C. water
- 2 C. chopped tomatoes
- 1/3 C. chopped fresh parsley
- 1 1/2 tsp salt
- 1/2 tsp dried thyme
- 1/4 tsp cayenne pepper
- 1/4 tsp ground black pepper
- 2 bay leaves
- 1/2 lb. cooked ham, cubed
- 1 (15.5 oz.) can black-eyed peas

Directions

- In a medium pan, heat 1/3 C. of the oil on medium-low heat.
- For the roux slowly, add the flour, beating continuously.
- Cook for about 5-7 minutes, beating continuously.
- In a large, heavy pan, heat 2 tbsp of the oil on medium-high heat and cook the okra, onion, celery and garlic for about 10 minutes.
- Add the roux and stir to combine well.
- Stir in the water, tomatoes, parsley, salt, thyme, cayenne pepper, pepper and bay leaves and bring to a boil.
- Reduce the heat and simmer for about 20 minutes, stirring occasionally.
- Stir in the ham and simmer for about 15 minutes.
- Stir in the black-eyed peas and simmer till heated completely.

Amount per serving (12 total)

Timing Information:

Preparation	30 m
Cooking	1 h
Total Time	1 h 30 m

Nutritional Information:

Calories	179 kcal
Fat	12.2 g
Carbohydrates	11.6g
Protein	6.4 g
Cholesterol	11 mg
Sodium	655 mg

* Percent Daily Values are based on a 2,000 calorie diet.

Traditional Southern Pancakes

Ingredients

- 1/2 C. butter or margarine
- 1/2 C. packed brown sugar
- 4 tbsps golden syrup or corn syrup
- 3 C. rolled oats
- 1/4 C. raisins

Directions

- Set your oven to 350 degrees before doing anything else.
- Mix the following in a big pan: syrup, sugar, and butter.
- Heat and stir the mix with a lower level of heat. Once everything is melted add your raisins and oats and continue stirring for 1 more min.
- Add everything to a square baking dish that is about 6 inches in length.
- Cook the oats in the oven for 35 mins. Then divide up the cake.
- Enjoy.

Amount per serving (10 total)

Timing Information:

Preparation	Cooking	Total Time
15 m	30 m	45 m

Nutritional Information:

Calories	250 kcal
Fat	10.8 g
Carbohydrates	36.7g
Protein	3.4 g
Cholesterol	24 mg
Sodium	75 mg

* Percent Daily Values are based on a 2,000 calorie diet.

COUNTRY MEAT LOAF

Ingredients

- 2 eggs, beaten
- 3/4 C. milk
- 1/2 C. dry bread crumbs
- 1/4 C. chopped onion
- 1 tsp salt
- 1 tsp ground black pepper
- 1/2 tsp crumbled dried sage
- 1 1/2 lbs ground beef
- 1/2 C. ketchup
- 2 tbsps brown sugar
- 1 tsp dry mustard powder

Directions

- Set your oven to 350 degrees before doing anything else.
- Get a bowl, mix evenly: sage, black pepper, whisked eggs, ground beef, salt, milk, onion, and crumbled bread.
- Get a 2nd bowl, combine: dry mustard powder, brown sugar, and ketchup.
- Enter meat into your loaf pan.
- Bake for 50 mins. Check that a temperature read out is 160 degrees internally.

- Remove the loaf from the oven and coat it with the wet mixture in your second bowl.
- Put meat loaf back in the oven and cook for another 10 mins.
- Let cool.
- Enjoy.

Servings: 5 servings

Timing Information:

Preparation	Cooking	Total Time
20 mins	1 hr	1 hr 20 mins

Nutritional Information:

Calories	388 kcal
Carbohydrates	22.2 g
Cholesterol	163 mg
Fat	20 g
Fiber	0.9 g
Protein	28.9 g
Sodium	935 mg

* Percent Daily Values are based on a 2,000 calorie diet.

THANKS FOR READING! JOIN THE CLUB AND KEEP ON COOKING WITH 6 MORE COOKBOOKS....

http://bit.ly/1TdrStv

 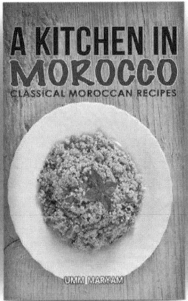 

To grab the box sets simply follow the link mentioned above, or tap one of book covers.

This will take you to a page where you can simply enter your email address and a PDF version of the box sets will be emailed to you.

Hope you are ready for some serious cooking!

http://bit.ly/1TdrStv

Come On...
Let's Be Friends :)

We adore our readers and love connecting with them socially.

Like BookSumo on Facebook and let's get social!

Facebook

And also check out the BookSumo Cooking Blog.

Food Lover Blog

86225524R00081

Made in the USA
Lexington, KY
09 April 2018